Roy —

wishing him a Merry
                    Christmas

from T. H. & Mary Wright.

Christmas 1913.

THE "SHOWN TO THE CHILDREN" SERIES
EDITED BY LOUEY CHISHOLM

BIRDS

PLATE I

Missel Thrush—(11 inches)

BIRDS

SHOWN TO THE CHILDREN

BY

M. K. C. SCOTT

DESCRIBED BY

J. A. HENDERSON

FORTY-EIGHT COLOURED PICTURES

LONDON & EDINBURGH

T. C. & E. C. JACK

TURNBULL AND SPEARS, PRINTERS, EDINBURGH

LIST OF BIRDS

TO
ALISON MARY OGILVIE

ABOUT OUR BIRDS

IN the life of a bird the changing seasons are
the great events, and each one brings with it
different duties, different conditions, and therefore
different ways of life. In winter most of the
birds are silent. They have no heart to sing in
the cold weather. Often food is hard to find,
and the search for it takes all their time in the
short days. At night they roost among the
bushes or in some quiet corner in their native
haunts. In many cases they crowd together,
poor shivering things, to keep warm; and some
birds use the shelter of their old nests. You may
be sure they welcome very eagerly the first sign
of spring and new life, and sing it in with all their
hearts: " Life again, light again, leaf again, love
again!" It is then that the flocks of birds that
have lived together since autumn separate into
pairs. They are supposed to choose their mates
on St Valentine's Day, the 14th of February.
Chaucer makes them sing to their mates:—

> " Blessed be Seynt Valentyne!
> For on his day I choose you to be myne
> Withouten repentyng, mine herte swete."

its surroundings. All these eggs are cared for
with anxiety by the parent birds, and kept warm
patiently for days, until the chicks are hatched.
Then they are busier than ever, for the young
birds grow so fast that they need a great deal of
food, and the parents are kept working late and
early to find the right kind for them. Then the
song-birds have little time for singing, and many
of them are altogether silent.

All birds show great care for their young ones,
and in case of danger many of them cleverly
devise ways of protecting them. A favourite way
is that of the Peewit, who limps away from the
nest pretending she is hurt and cannot fly. When
you follow her, thinking you can catch her, she
leads you right away from her treasure, and then
rises and flies off, whole and strong again.
Most birds utter loud cries of grief when their
young ones are endangered. Many are so devoted
to their charge that, when sitting on eggs, they
will rather allow themselves to be taken in the
hand than desert their brood. And surely no one
would take advantage of such faithfulness to
hurt in any way those brave little people.
Another remarkable thing to notice is the way in
which young birds, principally those that break
through to the light in exposed places, moors and

hillsides, know at once how to hide from danger. The young Snipe or Grouse will lie flat and keep quite still in the presence of an enemy, knowing, from the moment it leaves the egg, that thus it will be least seen.

When the young birds have been taught to fly, and can shift for themselves, the time of the summer moult comes on, and July is a very silent month, when one wonders where all the birds have gone. The singing is over for the year with most of them. The Skylark is silent and the Thrush and Blackbird; but the Willow-wren sings again in August with just a soft echo of his spring song; and the Robin gladdens the dreary autumn days and is more welcome then, when he is almost the only singer, than at any other time. The migratory birds collect in flocks, preparing for their journeys south, and in September the Swallows may be seen practising all day long, or sitting in rows on the telegraph wires, discussing their plans. By the end of October all the summer visitors have gone, and for the others, there is the bleak winter to face again.

So you see there is much of interest and beauty to watch in the ways of birds, and a great pleasure will be added to your country walks if you learn to see them. Cultivate an ear quick to distinguish

the different notes and to hear an unknown
one among many familiar sounds; and an eye
alert to see the least movement among the
branches and to notice with one glimpse, enough
of the form and colour of a passing bird to
recognise it.   Birds are difficult to see at first;
they will not sit still, like wild flowers, for you to
examine them.   But how infinitely more interesting and lovable they are, by all the life of them,
by the brains and hearts of them !

J. A. HENDERSON.

BIRDS
SHOWN TO THE CHILDREN

PLATE I.

THE MISSEL-THRUSH

IN the winter season most of our British birds are silent, or if a gleam of sunshine tempt them to a little burst of song, it is apt to be wavering and uncertain. But there is one bird who sings his best during the darkest and stormiest days of mid-winter. In a gale of wind and rain the Missel-thrush loves to sit on a high branch of some tall tree, pouring out his song when all other birds are driven into shelter; and thus he has earned the name of Storm-cock, which is often given him. His song lasts for several minutes at a time, without a break, then ceases, and begins again. He stops singing after mid-summer, and does not begin in earnest until Christmas is over, although he may be heard occasionally during autumn.

The Missel-thrush lives in woods and plantations, and any winter's morning may be seen in the fields at the edge of the wood, looking big in the mist. He is fond of orchards and gardens too, and may do a good deal of damage to fruit and berries in the autumn. His food is principally berries of all sorts, and he got his name because he was supposed to live chiefly on the berries of the mistletoe. But he also eats snails and insects and worms, and corn too, sometimes. He has a habit of moving in little sudden runs, and then suddenly stopping with head and beak raised as if listening most anxiously. When flying, he goes up and down on his way, but goes fast with quick beats of his wings.

In autumn, Missel-thrushes go about in little scattered parties of ten or twenty birds, not in close company, yet never very far apart. They utter a harsh, loud scream when any danger threatens, and as they are then exceedingly alert and wary, it is not easy to get very near them. The little flocks break up in January, and the birds pair, and then they become much less shy. The nest is made in a tree, such as an oak or elm, close to the trunk, and as it is a large structure, made of twigs, grasses, mud and wool, lined with soft grass, it is easily seen in the leafless branches. Four to six eggs are laid: they are usually of a pale green colour speckled with brown, but the colours vary a good deal.

PLATE II.

THE SONG-THRUSH

THIS is another kind of Thrush, called Song-thrush, because he sings more beautifully than the others; and he is sometimes called the Throstle. He is smaller than the Missel-thrush, being about nine inches long. His back and wings are brown, and his breast is of a pale yellow colour, with spots of dark brown all over: and when he flies you will see that his wings underneath are yellowish too. He is one of the commonest of our birds, and is to be seen usually near gardens, because there his food is most easily found. You will know him best by his song, as he is one of the very finest singers of all the birds. He will sit on the bare branch of a tree for a long time, singing, singing, singing, as if his heart were full of happiness, because it is spring and everything is so beautiful. He has a way of singing one or two or three notes, then repeating them, exactly the same, several times over.

About March the pair of birds find a safe place for their nest, in a thick hedge, or perhaps in some ivy against a wall, and not very far above the ground. Then they collect twigs and straws for the outside of their house. Inside they put

PLATE II

Song Thrush—(9 inches)

wet mud and moss and rotten wood and other soft things and work them all into a smooth lining; then the mud dries and it is all firm and strong and comfortable. There are about four eggs, bright blue with black spots. The Thrush feeds on all sorts of insects and worm and snails. You will see him on the lawn standing quite still with his head on one side, as if listening for a worm: then he will suddenly hop forward and pull one out of the earth. If he finds a snail and it goes into its shell, he will break the shell on a stone. He is very fond of fruit, too, and will come and eat strawberries in the garden.

The Thrush lays two or even three clutches of eggs in one year: and sometimes the first brood of chickens, having grown big, help to feed their little brothers. They stop singing about the end of June. You will not see many of them in winter, as they leave the garden and go away then.

PLATE III.

THE BLACKBIRD

"A birdie with a yellow bill
Hopped upon the window sill,
Cocked his shining eye and said,
Ain't you 'shamed, you sleepy head?"

THAT was a Blackbird, and a very wide-awake person he is: before the sun is up he is about, always smart and neat, with never a feather ruffled. The cock is quite black all over, except his bill, which is bright orange yellow. The hen is all dark brown with spotted breast and has no yellow bill. This bird is just a little bit bigger than the Song-thrush. In his ways he is very like him, and he, too, is a very fine singer. He has a rich, clear voice, and he will sing for an hour or two, straight on. The Blackbird does not repeat little groups of notes much, as the Song-thrush does, and so you will know one song from the other. He eats worms, listening for them, like the Thrush, and breaks the shells of snails. He will eat all the cherries and strawberries in the garden, if he is not kept off.

The Blackbird is quite common in all parts of the country, and is to be seen about gardens

PLATE III

Blackbird and Hen—(10 inches)

and shrubberies at any time of the year. If you come upon him suddenly, or startle him, he scuttles away with a great big noise, very much frightened. When he makes his nest, he chooses a hedge or evergreen bush to build in, and he begins like the Song-thrush with twigs and straws. Then he lines it all with mud, to make a hard wall; but inside the mud, he puts a soft lining of very fine grass and horsehair. In this cosy little home, about five eggs are laid: they are dull greenish blue, with blotches of brown. The hen is a very careful mother, and will sit close on her nest to protect her little ones, even if you come quite near and look at her, although it frightens her very much. Two or three times in each year she lays eggs. Sometimes the parent birds build a new nest each time, and sometimes they use the same one.

PLATE IV.

THE HOUSE SPARROW

WHEREVER we go we always have the Sparrow with us: even in the crowded streets he is to be seen, dashing down, almost under the horses' hoofs, for scraps of food. There, he is a grimy little person, and you cannot see his colours for the smoke has dimmed them. But round about cottages and farm-houses in the country he is very different, and the white bars on his wings are clear and distinct, and his cheeks and breast are soft pale grey, and his wings bright chestnut brown. The cock has a black chin and throat.

The Sparrow is very bold, fearless, and clever, but he is watchful and suspicious where human beings are concerned. Although he is constantly about our doors, and his cheerful chirping may be heard at any hour of the day, he does not make friends with man and trust him, as do the Robin and others of our favourites. Sparrows are very fond of company, however, and do all their business except nest-building, in little crowds, talking and arguing all the time. Like other birds, they take dust-baths to clean their oily feathers, and you will often see them on a dry road,

PLATE IV

House Sparrow—(6 inches)

spluttering dust all over themselves, as if it were water.

In the autumn when the grain is ripening they go in large parties to the fields. They are fond of grain and seeds of all kinds, and that is what they live on most of the year. They eat buds too, and many a seedling in the garden is nipped off by the Sparrows as soon as it shows a green tip above the ground. In summer they eat insects and caterpillars, and the young ones are fed on caterpillars.

Sparrows build in holes in walls, in a rainpipe, or in any sheltered nook about a house; and sometimes in trees. The nest is made of straw, moss, wool and feathers; and the eggs are five or six in number, dull white covered all over with blackish markings. As soon as one brood is reared and able to fly, another clutch of eggs is laid, and so on all through the summer.

The Sparrow is a cousin of the Finches, and like them, has a broad bill and a rather thick, heavy figure.

PLATE V.

THE CHAFFINCH

THE Chaffinch is the commonest of the Finches, and his loud, joyous song may be heard about the trees and hedges, fields and gardens, all through the summer months. He feeds principally on grain and seeds of various kinds, and with the Sparrows and the Greenfinches flocks of Chaffinches go to the fields when the farmer has sown his wheat; and later, when the harvest is taken in, they find food among the stubble. When the fields are ploughed again they go to the farm-steads and the roadside to find a living. In the summer they eat insects too, and they feed their young entirely on insects.

In April the hen builds a beautiful nest of fine grasses, and hairs and moss, cleverly woven together. She chooses them carefully and makes the nest look so like the tree or hedge in which it is placed that it cannot easily be seen. The hen does the building while the cock brings her the materials. She likes very much to decorate the outside with a scrap of something white, a bit of wool or tiny pieces of white lichen or the white bark of the birch.

The eggs number four or five, and are of a dull blue, spotted with reddish brown. In the autumn

PLATE V

K.S.

Greenfinch—(6 inches)

Chaffinch—(6 inches)

Hen

and winter, Chaffinchs go about in big parties, and sometimes you will see a crowd entirely of cocks, and sometimes one of hens only.

THE GREENFINCH

THE Greenfinch lives among trees and hedges, and it is often difficult to see his green and yellow feathers among the green leaves. And he has not the bright familiar song of the Chaffinch, so that although he is very common he is much less seen. He has a thicker neck and head than the Chaffinch and so looks heavier and not so neat.

The Greenfinch builds in evergreens and other thick bushes and hedges, and sometimes two or three pairs build their nests close together. The nest is of wool and moss lined with hair, and the eggs are of the palest blue spotted at one end with brown. The hen is a devoted mother, and has been known to devise a very cunning way of protecting her nestful of young ones, when she found they were too much exposed to the hot sun. She found some broad leaves and fixed their stems carefully into the rim of her nest, so that the leaves stood up round it and formed a sort of awning

PLATE VI.
THE BULLFINCH

THE Bullfinch is perhaps the most beautiful of his family, with his velvety black head and deep rich colours, and his particularly soft and silky feathers. He lives among trees, coming into gardens and orchards when the fruit-trees begin to show buds; and unless he is kept off he destroys all chance of fruit by eating the flower-buds. He eats ripe fruit too, and insects and seeds.

Like all the Finches, these birds are fond of bathing, and it is charming to see a pair, in some clear pool, flirting the water over themselves, then sitting on a branch, fluffing out their soft feathers and preening themselves.

The Bullfinch has a clear piping call-note, but his song in spring is very soft, a gentle warble which he sings to his mate for hours. He is sometimes captured and kept in a cage, and can be taught to whistle a simple tune.

He chooses his mate for life, and they stay together all the year round, and the young ones of one summer stay with them till the following spring. They build their nest rather low in some thick hedge or bush, making it of twigs and fine tough roots. Four or five eggs are laid, pale blue, spotted with brown.

PLATE VI

Goldfinch—(5 inches)   Bullfinch and Hen—(6¼ inches)

PLATE VI.

THE GOLDFINCH

THE Goldfinch is not now a common wild bird in this country, because so many are caught and kept in cages. But for that same reason he is a well-known bird. His colours are brilliant and beautiful, and he is a great favourite. He lives about lanes and orchards, as well as in open places where thistles grow; for his favourite food is the seeds of the thistle. It is delightful to watch a little party of Goldfinches hanging on to a group of thistles. They get into every position and are dainty and graceful in their movements. Always when they pull a seed from the thistle-head, they carefully pluck off the down before eating the seed.

The nest is made of moss, wool, hair, the down from the willow and other plants, and it is very beautifully woven together. It is placed in a fruit tree in a garden, or in a bush, often quite near to houses. The eggs are white, spotted with soft red, and they are four or five in number.

PLATE VII.

THE LINNET

THE Linnet is a bird that is much sought after as a cage-bird, because of his sweet song. He frequents open commons and moors, where furze-bushes are his favourite home. In the furze his nest is built, and in it he finds a roosting place, all the year round. Linnets like to live together in large parties, and even in the nesting season several may often be seen together. And perhaps their song is finest when several join together in a delicate chorus.

The Linnet lives on seeds of many different kinds of weeds, and he has his name from a word that means flax. The colours of this bird vary very much, and while the cock generally wears bright crimson on breast and forehead, some birds are without it, and some have yellow instead. The back is reddish-brown, and the wings and slightly forked tail are very dark, with white markings. They all lose the bright colours in winter. The hen bird never has the red breast.

The nest is made of twigs, roots, and moss, and lined with hair and a few feathers. Four to six eggs are laid, bluish-white with purplish spots.

PLATE VII

Linnet—(5½ inches)

Whitethroat—(5½ inches)

K.S.

PLATE VII.

THE WHITETHROAT

THE Whitethroat is one of the Warblers that make our woods and hedges glad with their songs in spring and summer, but leave us before winter to seek a kinder climate. He comes here in April, and then is to be met with in every thick-hedged lane. He is a restless little person, and moves on before you as you come, generally keeping on the other side of the hedge and out of sight but now and again pausing, to sing his quick, bright song. At another time, you may come quite close to him, when, heedless of your presence he sits in a bush, giving all his heart and mind to the business of his song. Some of his notes are very sweet and soft, others like the Sedgebird's "churr," harsh but still pleasing.

He searches about nettles and other tall weeds for caterpillars, and has been called "Nettle-creeper"; and he eats insects too, and both wayside and garden fruits.

The nest is a slender one of dry grasses, hair and down, placed low in a bush or on the ground among weeds, and the five eggs are greenish white and brown-spotted.

27

PLATE VIII.

THE REDBREAST

EVERYONE knows the Robin with his bright red breast and very bright black eye. In the summer he may be seen in every garden, hopping along half hidden by the shrubbery; or making little excursions on to the lawn, where he stands with wings half-drooped, now and then giving his tail a sudden little flirt. And in winter we see even more of him, for he comes close to our windows and even into the house, asking for crumbs, when snow lies on the hard ground. He reminds us of Christmas and of home, and that is why Englishmen all over the world remember and love Robin Redbreast more than any other bird.

But he does not live in gardens only. In the woods and thickets and hedges far away from houses you will meet him, for he is one of our very common birds. If you do not see him, you will hear him. He has a very beautiful song, clear and ringing, and in the spring-time when his song is at its very best, and he sings with all his heart and soul, no sound could be more gladsome and joyous. Sometimes two or three Robins will sing, each trying to outdo the others, till the

PLATE VIII

Redbreast—(5¾ inches)

wood rings with their music. Most birds are silent in the autumn and winter months, but not so the Robin. Except during the moulting time in the end of summer he sings all year, and on a cold damp day of late autumn it is a wonderful thing to hear his sudden burst of song, when a wandering ray of sunshine lights up the red and golden bramble leaves in some silent wood.

The Robin eats seeds, small berries and insects. The nest is built in a wall or bank, cunningly concealed. It is made of moss and leaves and sometimes is lined with hair. In it are laid five or six small greyish eggs spotted with pale dull red. The young Robins do not have the breast red at first, but speckled with brown; and very delightful bright-eyed little babies they are. They soon learn to feed themselves and the parents at last have to drive them away. Each pair of Robins keep their own little district for themselves and angrily resent any invasion of their territory. So when the young birds grow up, fierce battles occur between the old birds and the young to settle who shall have the quarters they are occupying.

PLATE IX.

THE NIGHTINGALE

THIS is one of the most famous of all birds in all countries, because of his beautiful song. He sings at night, and in the cool moonlight his wonderful liquid notes claim the attention the more because of the stillness all round. There is no other bird sound except perhaps the hooting of the brown owls or the chattering of some Sedge-birds by the river, their rasping notes showing by contrast the clearness of the Nightingale's tone. His voice is loud and ringing, every note round, and full and musical. This song has in it some notes so plaintive and others so thrilling with joy that it seems as if the Nightingale had deeper feeling and sympathy than other birds. Poets in all ages have tried to tell the meaning of his song, themselves singing beautifully of it.

The Nightingale, however, sings far more in the daytime than at night, but so many birds are singing then that he is less heard. He hardly ever sings when it is quite dark. The best time to hear him is an hour or two after sunset. But sometimes, on a warm summer's night, when the moon is shining, several birds will answer and sing to one another all night long.

PLATE IX

Nightingale—(6¼ inches)

The Nightingale spends the winter on the continent, coming to us about the middle of April. From then to the middle of June he sings constantly; but after that the young are hatched and he is so busy feeding them that he sings only occasionally and just for a short time. Some parts of the country he does not visit at all. He is not found in Ireland, nor in Cornwall or Devonshire, and he never goes so far north as Scotland.

The Nightingale is a small brown bird, very like a Robin in size and figure, and he has the same little ways. He droops his wings and jerks his head down and after two or three quick little hops he pauses for a little, just as the Redbreast does on the lawn. He lives oftenest in shrubberies, hedges and close plantations; and he eats worms, grubs and insects of various kinds. He is not very timid, and you can go quite near him when he is singing. The nest is placed on the ground under a bush, and is made of dead leaves and lined with grass, roots and hair. The four or five eggs are olive-brown.

PLATE X.

THE WILLOW-WREN

THE Willow-wren has no striking colours to attract the attention, but he is a pretty little bird, and a very friendly one. He is green on the back, soft greenish-yellow in front, and is quite small. His home is among trees, and you will often see him in bushy hedgerows by the roadside. He will allow you to go quite near and watch him as he goes about his business: perhaps flying from branch to branch calling to a baby-bird to follow, and teaching it to fly, or hunting for insects about the leaves of a tree. Often he will stop and trill out the sweetest little song in a beautiful soft voice, beginning at the top and coming down a few notes of a minor scale. He sings all through the summer and autumn, but his voice gets softer and softer. The Willow-wren goes away in September to escape the cold weather, and comes here in March or April. His nest is built in a bank or under a bush on the ground, and it is made with the opening at the side, and a roof to keep out the rain. About six delicate eggs are laid, white, with faint red speckles.

PLATE X

Sedge Warbler—(4½ inches)　　　Willow Wren—(4¾ inches)

PLATE X.

THE SEDGE-WARBLER

THE Sedge-warbler is brown on the back, and brownish-white underneath, and he has a yellow line over his eye. He lives beside lakes and marshes, among the sedges and reeds that grow by the water. As he does not often come to the top of the reeds he is difficult to see; but he can easily be heard, for he has quite a big song for so small a bird. One odd thing about him is that when he is disturbed he begins to sing loudly; and another is that sometimes he sings all night. His song is a kind of chatter, but it is very beautiful, and when you hear three or four of these little birds all round you singing together, they make a splendid chorus. The Sedgebird lives on insects that he catches on the top of the water, or as they fly. The nest is rather a big one, placed in a clump of coarse grass, and the eggs number about five, brownish-white, blotted all over with brown.

PLATE XI.

THE HEDGE-SPARROW

THIS is a very quiet little bird, of quiet colours and a soft little voice. His wings and back are brown with little streaks of darker brown, and his head and breast are dark grey, also streaked with brown. He has a way of suddenly shaking out his wings and so some people call him "Shuffle-wing." The Hedge-sparrow is not a cousin of the House-sparrow : his thin bill and neat figure are much more like those of the Robin. He sings very sweetly in the early months of the year, even before the winter is over : for he stays here all through the cold weather. He lives about hedges and bushes, in gardens and parks, and spends most of his time on the ground, looking for the seeds and small snails on which he feeds. He also eats insects and their eggs. In winter he comes close to the house for food, and becomes quite trustful and friendly. In a neat soft-lined nest in a hedge are laid four or five eggs of a beautiful clear sea-blue. The baby-birds are fed on insects.

PLATE XI

Hedge Sparrow—(5½ inches)   Spotted Flycatcher—(6 inches)

PLATE XI.

THE SPOTTED FLYCATCHER

THE Spotted Flycatcher comes to us for a short visit in summer, arriving in May and going off again in September. His back and head are brown, and his breast dull white with long spots of brown. He lives about parks and gardens and the borders of meadows, and he is always to be seen when he is near, for he never hides in the hedges or among the leaves of trees. What he likes is to be out in the open where he can see all the flies, and bees and such things that pass. He sits quite still watching for them, then when one comes he suddenly dashes at it, and catches it with a snap of his bill, and flies back to his perch again. Sometimes he may have quite a long chase, but he generally wins in the end. He builds his nest in all sorts of places—in a barn or a summer-house, most often in a bush or a tree against a wall: and he builds it of all sorts of things—grasses, mosses, straws, hairs, feathers. The five or six eggs are white or pale blue or green, generally spotted with red.

PLATE XII.

THE WREN

THE Wren is one of our commonest birds and a general favourite. He is everywhere; in our gardens, in wayside hedges, on heathery hillsides and on stony moors. He is easily known, for no one else is like this little red-brown bird, whose tiny tail stands straight on end. And certainly no bird so small has such a powerful voice. He sings beautifully, with clear round notes and a trill like that of a fine Canary.

The Wren builds a dome-shaped nest with a very small opening, in a bank or at the root of a tree, using dry leaves or moss and lining it with feathers and finer moss. Six to eight or more eggs are laid, pale with reddish spots; and when all the young Wrens are out in summer, the hedges seem full of them. The Wren lives on insects. In very cold weather he will sometimes come near houses for food, and will run along the ground close to a wall, searching every cranny, with tail and wings drooped, looking and moving very like a mouse. In winter, too, Wrens roost at night in their old nests for warmth.

PLATE XII

Nuthatch—(6 inches)

Wren—(3¾ inches)

PLATE XII.

THE NUTHATCH

THE Nuthatch is not so common as the wren, but he is one of the birds that will come near the house when food is scarce in winter, and may be seen from the windows. By putting small nuts in crevices about an old wall, you can attract him. He has a strong, sharp beak, with which he will hammer a nut till he breaks the shell and reaches the kernel. Like a Squirrel, the Nuthatch, when food is plentiful, sometimes hides a little store for hungry times.

This bird lives about trees, running up and down on the trunks and branches as easily as a fly on a wall. He runs, too, on the under side of branches, gripping the bark with strong claws. He eats insects, seeds and all kinds of nuts.

The nest is a hole in a tree. If the chosen hole is not big enough, the Nuthatch takes out wood with his hatchet-bill; and if the opening is too big, he is not at a loss, but plasters up the entrance, till it is of the right size. There, on a bed of dry leaves, five to seven eggs are laid, white, speckled with red.

PLATE XIII.

THE TREE-CREEPER

THOUGH one of our commonest birds, the Tree-creeper is yet not often noticed. He is rather a lonely bird, with no song but a little "cheep-cheep," and is much too busy attending to his affairs to waste time in play. His colours, too, are quiet and do not catch the eye. But if you are watchful, or looking specially for him, you are sure to find him in any wood. He is worth looking for, because his ways are unlike those of other birds, and he is not shy, so you can observe him closely without disturbing him. His life is spent on trees, not amongst the green leaves, but on the trunks and larger boughs, where the bark is cracking into little chinks and crevices. In these cracks live the insects and grubs on which the Tree-creeper feeds. His sober brown colour suits the colour of the trunks so well that he looks at first sight like a piece of bark; and his bill and claws and tail are all specially adapted to his business. The bill is long and slender and curved, so that he can probe easily into the smallest cracks in the bark; his strong claws hold him as he works along a trunk or the under side of a bough; and the feathers of

PLATE XIII

Treecreeper – (5 inches)

his tail are stiff and pointed, and help to support him as he moves upwards.

He has a regular plan of proceedings. Beginning at the foot of a tree, he creeps upwards, going round and round it, sometimes out of sight, sometimes in full view, wasting no time, but rapidly examining the bark all the way as he goes. Then perhaps he goes along a big branch, and when he comes to the end of the rough bark, he flies off down to the foot of the next tree and begins again. He sings very little at any time. In the spring he has a shrill call, and at other seasons he sometimes gives a faint little cheep as he flies from tree to tree.

The nest is made in a hole in a tree such as a pollard willow, or between the trunk and a loose piece of bark. It is neatly made of roots and twigs, grass and bits of bark, and is lined with wool and feathers. Six to nine little white eggs with red spots are laid.

PLATE XIV.

THE GREAT-TIT

THERE are several kinds of birds called Titmice or Tits, that are all like one another, and unlike other birds in their ways. They are all very restless and lively, and they can all hang up-side-down on the underside of a branch, just as easily as perch on the top of it.

The biggest of the Tits is the Great-tit, Tom-tit, or Oxeye. Back green, breast yellow, cheeks white, and head, collar, and a band down the middle of his breast black, he is a handsome, gaily-coloured bird. He is the same length as a Chaffinch, but his body is not so big. Insects and their eggs are his chief food, which he finds about the bark and leaves of trees. He eats seeds, too, and when they are hard he will hold them in his claws, and break them by tapping with his strong beak.

The Great-tit is not a shy bird; he visits gardens, and if you hang a bone on a tree, very likely he will come and eat the meat off it.

In spring the Great-tit has a loud, clear note. It sounds as if he called "Pink, pink."

The nest is built in a hole in an old tree or a wall, and is made of dry moss, and leaves and wool, and is lined with feathers. The white eggs

PLATE XIV

Great-tit—(6 inches)

Cole-tit—(4½ inches)

with brown spots number seven or eight. After
the little ones can fly, the Oxeyes go about in
little parties till the next spring.

THE COLE-TIT

THE Cole-tit has a black head and throat, white
cheeks and a white spot on the back of his
head: the rest of his body is grey above and
greyish-white underneath. He stays in the
woods more than the Great-tit, and he loves pine-
trees. You will see him best in the autumn or
winter when several fly about together, making
a little bustle in the tree-tops as they go. They
are never still a moment, but hurry about the
branches, any side up, looking for the insects they
like to eat: and they make little chirping notes
all the time. These parties of Cole-tits travel
about until the spring-time, when they pair, and
build nests. The nest, of moss and wool, is put
in a nook or cranny, like the nest of the Great-tit,
and the eggs, like those of the Great-tit too, are
white with brown spots, and number about seven
or eight.

F

PLATE XV.

THE BLUE-TIT

THE Blue-tit is a great favourite, perhaps because he is so friendly. He becomes very trustful, and will stay close to a window, eating meat or nuts that have been hung out for him, even while people are moving about inside the room. He has a bright blue crown and white cheeks, and a very dark line round his neck and through his eyes. His back and wings are greenish-blue, and the under parts are yellow. He is to be seen wherever there are trees and bushes, and he often does damage by pulling the buds off them in his search for insects, which he likes to eat: but he eats other kinds of things too, and is very fond of meat. The nest is made like the other Tits' nests, in all sorts of holes: sometimes the entrance is so very small, that you could hardly believe the birds could get in.

THE LONG-TAILED-TIT

Of all the little bands of Tits that wander about the tree-tops, none go with so much cheerful noise and bustle as the Long-tailed-tits.

PLATE XV

Long-tailed Tit—(5¾ inches)

Blue Tit—(4½ inches)

They have several notes—one, a little sound like "churr" is the most easily known. The Long-tailed-tit is black and white on head, back, and tail: at the top of the wing there is a patch of rosy red, and underneath the white is tinged with red. He has the softest and fluffiest of feathers. His beak is very tiny, and his tail is very long, and though his body is the smallest of all the birds in this country, his long tail makes him nearly as long as the Great-tit.

The Long-tailed-tit builds a wonderful nest in a tree or bush. It is made of moss and lichens woven together with fine wool and cobwebs, and has only a very small opening by which the birds can get in. Inside it is lined with a great many feathers, and altogether, it takes about three weeks to build. In it are laid eight or ten white eggs, speckled with red, and when the little birds come out, the whole family goes about together. You will sometimes see a row of six or more sitting huddled together on a branch, waiting to be fed by their parents, each a tiny ball of feathers at the end of its long straight tail. They are as pretty a family as you could meet on a long summer's day.

PLATE XVI.

THE SWIFT

THE Swift, the Swallow, and the two kinds of Martin are all alike in having very long wings and very short legs; and they all live on insects which they catch as they fly about. They do not go among trees and do not perch much, but spend nearly all their time on the wing. They cannot bear cold, and they go to Africa and other warm countries in August or September, coming back here only in April or May.

The Swift has the longest wings of all, and he flies round and round and about, all day long and even into the night. And while he flies he utters a harsh scream, so piercing that you can hear it even when the bird is almost out of sight.

The Swift is sooty black all over, except a white spot on his chin.

He lives about high buildings, and is particularly fond of church steeples and old towers. The nest is built in holes in walls, or in cliffs, or under the thatch of cottages. It is made of straws and feathers or anything suitable that the bird can find floating about in the air, for he never goes on the ground.

Two white eggs are laid.

PLATE XVI

K.S.

Swift—(8 inches)

Swallow—(7½ inches)

PLATE XVI.

THE SWALLOW

THE Swallow is bluish-black on the back and head and has a bluish-black bar across the breast; the under parts are white with a reddish tinge, and the throat and forehead are red. The tail is divided into two, like a fork, and is very long.

He lives near houses, building his nest in a chimney, or under the roof of a stable or outhouse, generally in a rather dark sheltered place. It is made of straw and wet earth, and lined with feathers.

Four eggs are laid, white with brown spots, and two broods are brought up in one summer. Sometimes you may see the mother feeding a young one while both are flying in the air.

The song is a little, soft, twittering sound.

Swallows fly almost as much as Swifts, and are often to be seen skimming over a river or lake because there are lots of insects there, sometimes going so close that they dip their wings in the water. When it is nearly time for them to go away for the winter, they gather in flocks and fly about together for days, preparing for their long journey over the ocean.

PLATE XVII.

THE HOUSE-MARTIN

THIS bird is very like the Swallow, with the same glossy black on wings and back: but the lower part of its back is white, and when you see them flying about together, you must look for that white bit, to know which is which. When they come near you will see, too, that the Martin has no black necklace, and no red parts, but is all pure white underneath. The legs and toes are covered with soft white feathers.

In all their ways, too, Martins are like Swallows. Like them they live near houses and on the walls they build their own homes. The nest is built of mud, and made to stick securely to the wall of a house, under the eaves, so that they shelter it from rain: and it is lined with feathers and soft grasses. They do not build a new nest each year, but just put a little fresh lining in their last year's home if it has not been damaged while they were away. So that often, year after year, the same nest will be occupied by one pair of birds. The hen lays two lots of four or five eggs, which are pure white.

PLATE XVII

Sand Martin—(5 inches)

House Martin—(5¼ inches)

K.S.

PLATE XVII.

THE SAND-MARTIN

THE Sand-martin is the smallest of the Swallow tribe, and is brown in colour, just a little darker than the sand it lives in. The under parts are white with a band of brown across the breast. The Sand-martin does not live beside houses, but chocses a sand-bank, often beside a river, or in a railway cutting. There with his tiny bill he digs a little hole and makes a narrow tunnel into the sand, two or three feet long, with a wider part at the end in which the nest is made of dry grass and feathers. The tunnel is made to slope up from the entrance, so that rain cannot get in to make the nest damp. The birds only work at the nest in the morning, and spend the rest of the day flying about and feeding, so that it takes them many days to finish it.

When a pair of those tiny Martins have made their nest, however, they do not have all that hard work to do over again, but come back to the old hole next year. They lay four or five delicate white eggs, twice in each year.

PLATE XVIII.

THE PIED WAGTAIL OR WATER WAGTAIL

AS soon as you see this bird you know who he is for he tells you his name by wagging his tail all the time!

He is black and white all over in summer, with white cheeks and forehead, and black chin and throat; but in winter he changes and becomes grey instead of black on the back and his chin and throat become white. In length he is between a Blackbird and a Chaffinch, but nearly half his length is his tail. He lives most near water, and is often seen running about the sea-shore, or flying with his up-and-down flirting motion from stone to stone in some little tumbling stream. He comes to meadows and gardens, too, and will bring his whole family in summer to your lawn, where they all run about looking for insects, the wind blowing up their long, straight tails. They are very light, and seem as they run as if they hardly touched the ground. These birds live on seeds, worms and insects, often chasing a gnat, in mid-air, with quick twists and turns. They sing a tiny warbling song. The Wagtail lays five or six

PLATE XVIII

Pied or Water Wagtail—(7¼ inches)   Grey Wagtail—(7¾ inches)

eggs, pale blue speckled with brown, in a nest of dry grass and moss, lined with wool and hair. It is built in a hole in the ground or in a wall or rock.

THE GREY WAGTAIL

THE Grey Wagtail is not so common as the Pied. He lives almost entirely about water, and likes best a mountain stream, where he runs over the rocks and about the water's edge, sometimes wading in the water. Whenever he stands for a moment, his tail goes up and down.

His back and wings are grey, his throat velvet-black and under parts clear, bright yellow. His tail is very long, longer than the Water Wagtail's, and it is black and white, tipped with yellow. He is one of the most beautiful of all our birds, and very charming to watch, being particularly graceful and dainty in all his movements. This bird's nest is made in a hole in a rock or on the ground under a rock, and five brown-speckled eggs are laid.

There is another Wagtail, the Yellow Wagtail, with more yellow about it, and no black on its throat, that is oftener seen than the grey in the South of England, while in Scotland the grey is much the commoner.

G

PLATE XIX.

THE WHEATEAR

THIS is a very common bird in open waste places : he loves desolate mountain-sides and stones. When you go for a walk in the country where there are no trees, you will often see him flitting along in front of you, and perching on a fence by the wayside. You will notice a flash of white, as he flies : that is the top of his tail, which is bright, clear white. His breast is white too, and a little stroke over his eye ; and round his eye is a black patch, and his wings and the end of his tail are black. His back is soft grey. The hen is a different colour, and in the autumn the cock gets more like her and the grey of his back changes to light brown, and his breast to palest brown. Sometimes as he sits on the top of a stone, he will dip his wings for a moment and spread out his tail like a fan. Sometimes he will dash at a passing fly. He eats flies, grubs and beetles. He goes to warmer countries for the winter, starting in August, and comes back here in March. From four to seven pale blue eggs are laid, in a nest made in a nook among stones, or in a hole in the ground. It is made of dry

PLATE XIX

Stonechat—(5¼ inches)
Wheatear Hen

Wheatear—(6½ inches)

grass and moss, and sometimes wool, for there are often sheep in those open places where Wheatears live. The Wheatear makes a little sound like "chat-chat," and sings a very little.

THE STONECHAT

THE Stonechat loves the open too, but places where there are whins and brackens, not stones. He is called "Stonechat" because he makes a little noise that sounds like two stones being knocked together. His head, throat, back and wings are black, and the top of his tail, like the Wheatear's, white; also his neck at the sides, and a bar on his wings are white; he has a beautiful rusty red breast. He always perches on the top of a fern or bush, and so you see his bright colours very clearly, but he never stays still long. The Stonechat builds a very neat little nest close to the ground under a furze-bush, and the eggs are pale green speckled with brown at one end. He sometimes sings, but his song is a very tiny one. He stays in this country all the year round.

PLATE XX.

THE COMMON BUNTING

THE Common Bunting, or Corn Bunting as it is often called, is a rather dull, clumsy bird with a monotonous voice and heavy movements. You may see him all over the country, in hedgerows or on the tops of brambles or tall weeds, and in winter large numbers collect together in the fields. His favourite perch is on a telegraph wire, and on a hot summer's day he will sit there for an hour at a time, uttering his song at regular intervals. The song is not very musical. It consists of two or three repetitions of the same note, followed by a sound like a mixture of several notes all uttered at once and not very unlike the noise of breaking glass. The Corn Bunting eats seeds of all sorts, and insects. He is especially fond of grain, and wanders over the fields after the corn is cut, and visits the hayricks and farmyards, picking up the fallen grains. The nest is placed in long grass, and is made of hay and roots, and lined with horsehair and fibres. Four to six eggs are laid, grey, with brown or purple spots or ash-coloured streaks.

PLATE XX

K.S.

Yellow Hammer—(6¼ inches)   Common Bunting—(7½ inches)

PLATE XX.

THE YELLOW-HAMMER

THE Yellow-hammer is very common everywhere in Britain, and is much more graceful and interesting than the Corn Bunting. He too is fond of sitting on the tops of hedges or bushes, and is easily recognised by his bright yellow head. He often sits still, till you are quite close to him, then flies on a little way, and waits for you to come up again. His song is a very familiar sound in the summer. It consists of two notes, the first repeated several times and the second, which is a little lower, uttered only once. It sounds quite like the words "A little bit of bread and no cheese," if you say the first words quickly in the same tone, and the last one more slowly and lower. All through the hottest, dustiest days the song comes through the air at regular intervals the bird sitting on a rail or twig for a long time at a stretch. It is a pleasant sound in the heat when most birds are silent. The nest is built on or near the ground under a clump of grass, and is made of hay and grass lined with horsehair. Three to six eggs are laid, dull purplish-white, streaked with purple veins.

PLATE XXI.

THE CUCKOO

THIS is a very strange bird indeed, and in his nature different from every other. He is a great favourite with mankind, and his voice is heard with gladness as a sign of the coming of summer. "Cuckoo, Cuckoo" he will call for an hour at a time, from the edge of a wood, or perched on a fence on the open meadow that he loves.

The strangeness of his habits, which makes him interesting to us, makes him feared and disliked by other birds. For the Cuckoo builds no nest of his own, but, when the hen has laid one of her dull grey eggs she carries it in her bill to some small bird's nest, and leaves it there—perhaps in a Wagtail's or a Hedge-sparrow's nest; most often in that of a Meadow-lark.

Now, the Cuckoo is a big bird, about the length of a Jackdaw, but she lays very small eggs, and so when she puts one beside the eggs of those smaller birds, they do not know that it is not one of their own. But as soon as the young Cuckoo is hatched there is trouble, for he has not even opened his eyes when he begins to want the nest all to himself, and throws out the eggs and baby

54

PLATE XXI

K.S.

Cuckoo—(13½ inches)

birds that really belong to it. This he does by getting underneath them; then, lifting them on his back, which is broad and hollow for that purpose, he rises to the edge, and tumbles them out. He grows very fast, and wants such lots of food that he keeps his foster-parents as busy as if they had their own whole brood to care for. After he is able to fly they still feed him for several weeks. Always they are most devoted to their strange changeling, and work for him untiringly even when he has grown to be twice their size. You may see a little Meadow-lark perch on the shoulder of her big Cuckoo-baby, while she puts caterpillars into his mouth.

When the old Cuckoos start in August for a warmer country, the young ones are not yet able for the journey; so they follow in September, finding the way by themselves.

The Cuckoo is grey, with spots of white on the tail; and white underneath, with dark bars. The young bird is brown, and his greedy open mouth shows bright orange inside.

PLATE XXII.

THE CORNCRAKE

THE Corncrake or "Land-rail" is a very common
bird in this country, but he is very seldom
seen. He lives usually in fields of corn or hay,
and seldom leaves them, running about between
the stalks and finding all his food without coming
out to more open places. He is safe in there, for
the farmer will not let you walk through his hay or
corn to frighten the bird out. And even when he is
continually uttering his peculiar cry it is not easy to
say just where he is. The note is one of the most
familiar sounds we hear in summer. A continual
monotonous "crek-crek," which goes on without
change most of the day and all evening, and
sometimes much of the night as well. If you
stand by the field, the sound seems to be coming
from one place, and just when you have decided
that the bird is in one particular corner, "crek-
crek" it comes from the other side, until you cannot make out where he is at all. Very likely he
is all the time nearly in the same place, but can
make the sound seem to come from different
places. Perhaps, though, he really does run very
quickly from place to place. His body is long,
and his head shaped like a wedge, so that he can

56

PLATE XXII

Corncrake —(11 inches)

hurry through the thick corn or grass at a great rate. Sometimes, in wild waste parts of the country, he lives among tufts of rushes. From such places it is not so difficult to drive him out, and you may then see him running very fast along the ground, or flying to shelter, if closely chased. He lives on insects, worms, snails, and seeds.

The Corncrake is not a very small bird, being nearly as big as a Partridge; and he is more brightly coloured. On the back the feathers are yellowish-brown with dark centres, and the wings are chestnut. The throat is white, the breast greyish or buff, and the flanks are streaked with broad bars of brown and buff. He has ashy grey patches above the eyes and on the cheeks.

The nest is made of dry grass and leaves, and is placed in growing corn or grass. It holds seven to ten eggs, reddish-white with spots of bright brown and grey.

H

PLATE XXIII.

THE SKYLARK

EVERYONE knows the song of the Skylark. With all sorts and conditions of men it is the favourite among the glad sounds of early spring. The Lark begins to sing very early in the year, as soon as bright days in February have given him the least encouragement. But as the sun becomes more powerful, the song is finer and more frequent, and through early summer it ceases only on the stormiest days. Very early in the day, too, he begins, and even on the longest day he is up before the sun. " Hark, hark, the lark at Heaven's Gate sings," Shakespeare said; and truly it sounds as if sheer joy carried him there always, to give thanks because it is so good to be alive. As he sings he soars up and up and up until the eye can follow him no further; then gradually coming down again he sings until he is close to the ground, dropping to his nest "those quivering wings composed, that music still." If there is any sign of danger he goes down not directly to his nest, for if he did that would tell his secret of where it is, but into the grass some little distance away.

The nest is built in a hole such as is made by a

PLATE XXIII

K.S

Skylark—(7¼ inches)

horse's hoof, or under a tuft of grass in a field or meadow. It is made of dry grasses and holds four or five eggs, darkly mottled on a whitish surface. Two or three broods are reared in one season. Choosing, as the Lark does, to build his nest among grass, he sometimes has the misfortune to have it disturbed at the hay-harvest. In such a sad plight, the birds have been known to carry their young ones in their claws to a safer place; or if the nest is not altogether destroyed, they may mend it and stay in their old quarters.

The Skylark has back and wings mottled with different shades of brown, and the breast is yellowish, with long brown spots. The feathers on the top of the head, he sometimes raises to form a crest. He lives always on the ground or in the air, hardly ever perching on hedge or bush. His food is small insects and caterpillars, and seeds and the tender blades of grasses. In autumn Larks gather together in large flocks and live together till spring.

PLATE XXIV.

THE MEADOW-PIPIT

THIS little brown bird you may very easily mistake for a Skylark, for the two are much alike in colouring; both have long dark spots on the breast, and both may be seen running about the ground to find food. Indeed, the Pipit is sometimes called "Meadow-lark," and "Titlark" is another of his names. He is considerably smaller, however, and is without the crest that the Skylark wears. He lives about fields and open places, commons and moors, and often he is the only small bird to be seen on a lonely hillside. You will very often meet him going quietly about country roadsides; and as you come along he will move off, a few yards at a time, with a jerky flight, always keeping a little ahead of you, and seeming interested in your movements, but so little afraid that he will let you come quite close.

The Pipit lives on small beetles, worms, insects and seeds, so most of his time is spent seeking for them on the ground. He does not perch on trees. The nest is rather large, but neatly made in a hollow in the ground or under a tussock or low bush. Grass, fine roots, and hair are used. The five eggs are brown, mottled with darker shades.

PLATE XXIV

K.S.

Rock Pipit—(6¾ inches)   Meadow Pipit—(5¾ inches)

The Tit-lark is not a great singer, but in spring he utters a pleasing little song as he drops slowly down from a height in the air, with wings and tail outspread.

THE ROCK-PIPIT

THE Rock-pipit lives on the seashore and is common all round our rocky coasts. He is larger than the Meadow-pipit and darker in colour, his back being a dark green-brown that does not show readily against his native rocks. He lives on little marine insects and worms and constantly runs about seeking them in crevices in the rocks, or among the seaweed left uncovered by the falling tide. When he stands he sometimes moves his tail up and down like a Wagtail. His ordinary note is a shrill "Peep," but in spring his little warbling song is like the Meadow-lark's and is sung when the bird is in the air.

The Rock-pipit's nest is made among dry seaweed, or in a sheltered place under a rock, or among bents by the seashore. It is made of dry grasses and seaweed, and the four or five eggs are of a greenish colour, spotted with brown.

PLATE XXV.

THE STARLING

THE Starling has increased in number greatly of recent years, and, as he likes to live near human beings, is now one of our most familiar birds. He is not a graceful bird, but in spring, when his glossy coat is at its best, and the dancing purple and green are reflected from his dark feathers, he is beautifully coloured. At most times of the year the glossiness looks oily, and his noisy, quarrelsome, greedy habits have little attractive in them.

He is fond of the company, not only of his own kind, but of other birds, and is rarely seen alone. After the young birds are able to take care of themselves, the Starlings begin to collect in flocks of varying size, and visit the feeding grounds in companies. Their food consists chiefly of worms, insects and beetles, and they visit the seashore, and also perch on the backs of sheep in the search. When autumn approaches, they eat berries and small fruit of all kinds; and a flock of thousands of Starlings will remove every cherry from an orchard in a very short time.

They like to roost together in crowds, and come night after night to the same place. From

PLATE XXV

Starling—(8½ inches)

all sides, huge companies of birds collect, till there are many thousands of them on the trees, all chattering, screaming, calling at one time. Now and again the huge flock rises into the air like a dark cloud, wheels round, and returns to the trees, while the noise of the voices and the wings is incessant and distracting. This babel lasts for perhaps an hour, then all at once the birds settle to roost, and in five minutes there is complete silence.

The Starling has no song of his own, but he will sit on a ledge or chimney for an hour at a time pouring out the oddest mixture of chuckling, whistling, and croaking sounds, in which fragments of the calls and songs of many other birds are imitated exactly. He is a very clever mimic, and can even be taught to whistle tunes. The nest is made in a hole in a tree, cliff, barn or wall, and is composed of grass and moss, and sometimes lined with wool. The five eggs are of a pale green-blue, and at first the young birds are grey-brown in colour.

PLATE XXVI.

THE ROOK

EVERYONE knows the Rook. He is the largest of our very common birds, and his deep black colour as he stalks across the grass, and his noisy cawing as he attends to his household compel us to notice him.

Most birds at breeding time avoid the society of all others except their mates, but the Rook likes the company of other Rooks at all times, and the rookery is one of the most familiar of sights. Early in the year the birds begin to pay occasional visits to the old nests to see how they have stood the winter's storms. By the end of February or the beginning of March house-building begins in earnest. The old nest must be repaired or a new one built, and as it all requires much discussion, and disputes are frequent, a rookery is one of the noisiest, cheeriest places possible. At that time the trees have no leaves, and the big nests, built at the very top of the highest trees, are easily seen. Rooks seem to like to build near houses, and they come back to the same place year after year. Four or five eggs are laid, bluish-green, with purple and brown spots. In winter, the birds from several rookeries often roost together, separating during the day-time to search for the worms and grubs and grain on which they live.

Plate XXVI

Jackdaw—(13 inches)

Rook—(18 inches)

PLATE XXVI.

THE JACKDAW

THE Jackdaw you can easily recognise anywhere. He is a little like the Rook in his glossy black plumage, and is often seen in company with him. But he is smaller and different in figure, and the grey patch on the nape and on the back of the head is not difficult to see. He is a pert, active, bustling fellow, always full of life and spirits, and very fond of the company of other birds. Usually several Jackdaws live near one another, sometimes hundreds, and their loud shrill caws are cheerful to hear. They do not like to build on the branches of trees, but prefer a rocky cliff or a stone building upon which to rest the nest. The inside of a church belfry or a ruined tower is a very favourite place, and sometimes enormous quantities of sticks and twigs are dropped into a staircase or a hole in the masonry to make a suitable level place for the nest. This is lined with wool, hair, and feathers; and the eggs, three to six in number, are pale green-blue, spotted with brown.

PLATE XXVII.

THE MAGPIE

HANDSOME, gay and clever, inquisitive, mischievous and a great chatterbox, the Magpie is full of character.

In this country he has an enemy in the gamekeeper, because he does a little damage by eating the eggs and young of game-birds, and so he is not allowed to be very common. And having this enemy, the Magpie has become very shy and wary, and lives about woods, building his nest generally in very high trees. In countries where he is always kindly treated he lives in a bush or tree close to houses and becomes very friendly.

He is a beautiful bird, black and white all over, the black on wings and tail showing brilliant green, blue and purple reflections in the sunlight. The tail is very long, and when the bird flies it is spread out and you see its beautiful shape, the feathers getting shorter and shorter from the central ones outward. It is often moved up and down like that of a Wagtail. The Magpie hops about on the ground, taking great long leaps and sudden darts, now this way and now that. He is looking for grubs, worms, and snails, and he probably does more good to the farmer by eating them, than any harm he does the gamekeeper by eating eggs.

PLATE XXVII

K.S.

Jay—(13½ inches)

Magpie—(18 inches)

The Magpie makes a clever nest of sticks and mud, layer upon layer, lining it with fine roots: over that a roof of sticks is built, leaving an opening just big enough for him to get in by; and round the opening and over the whole nest, as a defence against enemies, are many long sharp thorns. In this safe home the hen lays six eggs, brown-spotted all over, and she guards them bravely.

The chatter of the Magpie is harsh and unmusical, but a cheerful sound none the less.

THE JAY

THE Jay lives in woods where there is undergrowth, and, cleverly hiding among the foliage, is not easily seen. But he proclaims his presence by his loud chattering and screaming. He is gaily coloured: light brown, black and white, with blue eyes and part of the wing barred with bright blue. His black and white crest he can raise at will. He builds an open nest in a bush or tree, and five or six brown-speckled bluish eggs are laid.

The Jay is fond of acorns and other nuts; he also eats insects, worms, young birds and eggs, and sometimes mice.

PLATE XXVIII.

THE WOOD-PIGEON

DURING the spring and early summer the soft "coo-coo" of the Wood-pigeon, or Ring-dove, as it is also called, can be heard murmuring constantly in the wood; and at these seasons the birds can often be seen perching in the trees or flying close at hand. In autumn and winter they are much more shy and timid, and it is not at all easy to get close to them in the daytime. Towards evening they collect together, and as they choose the same trees each night to roost upon, one can come near them even in autumn by waiting close to their favourite resting-place. They like to sit near the tops of the tallest trees, and are specially fond of larch and fir plantations. Often before perching they clap their wings together, making a sharp sound, which can be heard quite a long way off. If suddenly startled, they fly out with a great flapping of wings and noisy disturbance amongst the branches.

The Wood-pigeon feeds on all sorts of grain, and seeds and berries, and in cold hard winter even on roots and turnip leaves. Sometimes at good feeding-grounds, great flocks of hundreds of birds collect from far and near. You may hear

PLATE XXVIII

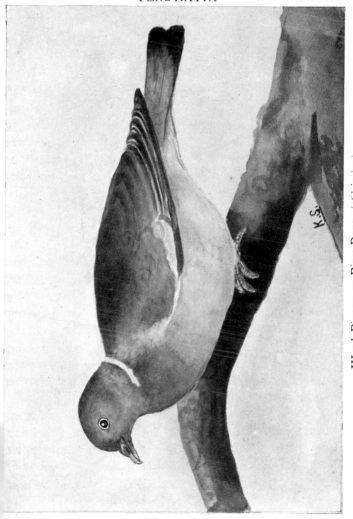

Wood Pigeon or Ring Dove—(16½ inches)

their wings whistling in the air as they come, then they make a turn in the air, and drop quickly to the ground. They have a habit of moving the head from side to side as they walk.

In spring the male has a special little dance, which he performs to please the hen bird. Approaching her with little hops, flirting his wings and spreading his tail, he suddenly rises up into the air, and swoops down again with a graceful motion, very pretty to watch. At other seasons he is not very attractive, although his colours are soft and rich.

The nest is loosely made of sticks, and placed high up in a tree. Two eggs of a pure glossy white are laid, and two broods are reared in the season. When the young are hatched, they are fed with a pulpy substance made from grain and seeds by the parents; and the young birds feed themselves by putting their bills deep into the parent's mouth and drinking this "pigeon's milk," as it is called.

PLATE XXIX.

THE BARN-OWL

THE Owl looks so grave and solemn that he has always been taken as a symbol of wisdom. He looks at you straight, not sideways with one eye at a time like other birds. And round each eye is a great circle of soft feathers, almost like big spectacles, that makes him look so serious, and rather shocked and surprised! Those big eyes are very wonderful, for they can see in the dark, and see so well that the Owl can drop on a mouse in a field, from quite high up. But daylight is too strong for them, so he sleeps by day and flies about and hunts at night.

The Barn-owl is the commonest kind, in this country. He has been called so because he likes to live in barns, where rats and mice come for grain; and the Barn-owl lives mostly on rats and mice. Instead of a barn, he sometimes chooses a belfry tower, or an ivy-clad ruin or perhaps a hollow tree. He sits upright, sleeping, all day, but on the slightest sound an eye is opened, and if a mouse moves in the half-dark barn, he drops on it silently and seizes it in his talons. Then he swallows it whole! And the skin and bones he afterwards throws up in round pellets. He

PLATE XXIX

K.S.

Barn Owl—(14 inches)

sometimes eats small birds and at night they are afraid of him ; but if he goes out in daylight, they often chase and annoy him.

This bird has a second name, the White-owl, because of his pure white under plumage; his tawny back, too, is spotted with white and his face is white. His face is heart-shaped when he is awake, but becomes much longer and narrower when he is seated on his perch with closed eyes. All Owls have remarkably soft, fluffy feathers.

Yet another name, the Screech-owl, he has earned by his strange, low, rasping note. So eerie it sounds in the dark that people in all ages have taken it for tidings of woe, and been frightened by it. The Screech-owl hisses too, and the young ones make a snoring sound, calling for food. It is another bird, the Brown-owl, that hoots " Tu-whit, Tu-whoo."

On a nest of a few sticks, the Barn-owl lays five or six rough, white eggs. She lays first two or three ; then a few days later, other two or three, so that the young birds of a nest are all of different ages.

PLATE XXX.

THE KESTREL

THIS is the commonest of our Hawks, and is easily recognised. He flies quickly at no great height above the ground, with rapid movement of the wings, watching the field and hillside beneath him for his prey. Suddenly he stops short and hangs motionless over one place, the tail spread out, and the wings now quite steady, now rapidly beating; and he remains poised or hovering in this way for quite a long time. He may then swoop down a little and again stop; and then dart down upon a mouse or other dainty, or else rise up and fly off to some other spot. So characteristic is this habit that he is as often known by the name of "Wind-hover" as by that of Kestrel. No other bird is like him in this. Kestrels live on field mice and small birds of all sorts; they eat large insects too, and sometimes frogs. They make their nests in cliffs or towers, and sometimes in holes in trees or rocks. The nest is very simply made and holds four to six eggs. They are of a reddish-white colour, covered nearly all over with red spots and blotches.

PLATE XXX

Kestrel—(15 inches)

Sparrow Hawk—(12 inches)

PLATE XXX.

THE SPARROW-HAWK

THE Sparrow-hawk likes cultivated country, where there are woods and hedges. In such districts it is easy to find small birds, and these are her chief food, although she sometimes eats mice too. The hen is much larger than the cock, and both are fierce, active birds, very light and graceful in their movements. They frequently perch on some projecting stone or bough and sit very upright with the eager eyes scanning the country round. The flight is smooth and easy, and a Sparrow-hawk skimming along the hedge or side of a wood, with wings sometimes motionless, sometimes quickly beating, often steals upon an unsuspecting little bird so quickly and suddenly that it is too frightened to make any attempt at escape. When chasing a bird in the air, she can turn and double so quickly that its only chance of safety is to take refuge in some thick bush or hiding-place.

The nest is built of twigs and is round and large. Sometimes a Magpie's old nest is used. Four or five bluish-white eggs are laid, marked chiefly at the larger end with red-brown blotches.

PLATE XXXI.

THE GOLDEN EAGLE

THE Eagle is the king of birds, just as the Lion is the king of beasts. No other of our birds is his equal in size or strength or fierceness, and he lives in wild and lonely places far away from houses and men. He is not a common bird now. Many years ago, he was much less rare, but gamekeepers have shot so many of the parent birds and destroyed so many of the nests that very few are left alive.

The Golden Eagle gets his name from the golden-red feathers of his head and neck and legs; but sometimes the colour is very dark, almost black. He is found chiefly in Ireland and Scotland, in the high mountainous districts of the mainland and on the islands and sea-coast of the west and northwest. There he is often seen, high up near the summits of the hills and crags, wheeling round and round in slow wide circles, guiding himself by his tail and scarcely moving his broad wings, which are stretched out with the tips a little turned up. The wings may measure more than eight feet from tip to tip, and his body is over three feet long.

He lives on smaller birds, such as grouse, and

PLATE XXXI

Golden Eagle—(36 inches)

on rabbits, hares and other small animals. These he chases out into the open, and then sweeping down grips them with his strong claws and carries them away. Sometimes he may even carry off a lamb, when there are hungry young ones in his nest. The old birds often hunt together, one flying slowly close along the hillside, frightening out their prey, while the other floats above and catches any bird or beast that tries to escape. They have been seen to drive a young red deer over a precipice by flapping their wings round its head, till it ran bewildered over the edge. Eagles pluck off the fur with their hooked bills, before they eat the animal they have caught.

The nest is made on a sheltered ledge of some high and rocky cliff, far above the ground, and often in so secure a place that no one can reach it, unless lowered by a rope from above. Sometimes only a few sticks are laid together, but some nests are large structures of twigs and heather and grasses. Two or three eggs are laid, greyish-white with rusty-brown blotches all over. The same nest is used year after year if the birds are not disturbed.

PLATE XXXII.

THE KINGFISHER

HAVE you ever been walking along the banks of a sheltered river and seen flash past you close to the water a brilliant little bird all green and blue and gold ? It was a Kingfisher, the most brightly coloured of all our British birds. You are not likely to have seen more of him than just a glimpse of his dazzling colours as he passed, for he is very shy and watchful. Unless you are very quiet, and specially looking for him, he will see you coming and be off before you can get close. When once you have found him, though, you will be able to find him again. He keeps always to the same stretch of water, where he fishes for his food ; and if you watch him carefully and often, you will find that he has his favourite places where he likes to come and perch. He lives on minnows and other small fish which he catches by diving. He sits on an overhanging bough or stick, watching the water ; or else he hovers above the surface, if there is no convenient perch. When a fish swims under him he plunges head first right into the water, and comes up with it in his beak. He kills it by beating it against his perch, and then swallows it head first.

76

PLATE XXXII

Kingfisher—(7¼ inches)

He lives on the banks of streams and rivers, mostly inland, but sometimes close to the sea and the salt water.

The nest is made in a hole. Sometimes the birds use a hole which they find under a tree-root, but sometimes they have to dig one in an over-hanging bank; and it may be quite a long way from the water, though it is generally beside it. The hole is made two or three feet deep, and slopes upwards from the entrance. A Kingfisher's nest is very difficult to find. It is made of the oddest substance you could think of; for it is of fish-bones. This little bird is unable to digest the bones of the fish it swallows, so it brings them up again into its mouth and throws them out. Owls do the same thing with the fur and bones of the animals they eat, and so do some other birds. At nesting-time the Kingfishers carry all these bones into the hole they have chosen, and piling them together make that their nest. Six to eight round white eggs are laid.

PLATE XXXIII.

THE DIPPER

THIS is a very interesting bird, because, although he is a land-bird, he goes under the water for his food. He is a little smaller than a Song-thrush; his tail is quite short and often stands up like a Wren's tail; he is black, all but his throat and breast, which are pure white. He lives beside rivers—stony rivers that flow fast and have little falls and rapids as well as quiet pools. When he perches on the stones he keeps bobbing his tail up and down and dipping his body. His call is a short, clear piping note and in spring he sings very sweetly. He lives on insects and the eggs of water insects and of small fish, and to find these he walks right into the water and underneath. No one knows quite how he manages to stay under, but he makes his wings go as if he were flying, which helps him, and he moves along the bottom of the river finding his food. Now and then of course he has to come up to breathe, then he sinks in again. It is very strange that he should be able to go about in the water, because he has not webbed feet like the duck, to swim with, so he must either walk, or swim with his wings. Sometimes he floats on the top of the

78

Plate XXXIII

Dipper—(7 inches)

water, spreading his wings. And where water
falls over a rock, he will dash through it, just for
fun.

Each pair of Dippers has a particular part of a
river which they keep for their very own, and will
not allow other Dippers to come near; then further
up the river another pair will have another part
for their own, and so on. And when a Dipper
goes up a stream before you, flying from stone to
stone, he will only fly to the end of his own bit
of country, then pass you and go down again.
The Dipper builds a big nest under the river
bank, or among stones, and it is made with a
roof. Four white eggs are laid, and the little
birds can go about in the water almost before they
can fly. When their own river freezes in winter,
the Dippers go to other places where there is
water, but they stay in this country all the year
round.

PLATE XXXIV.

THE SAND-PIPER

THE Sand-piper is common in this country during spring and summer. He lives about rivers and the margins of lakes, always making his presence known by his loud clear note. He is very active, running nimbly about the rocks, wading in the water, swimming, and sometimes diving in search of the worms and insects on which he lives. He is very wary and will not allow you to get near him. He will watch an intruder from far off, and taking his stand perhaps on a stone in the middle of the broad river, will repeat again and again his clear, piercing note, bobbing his tail up and down the while, anxious and alert to fly off at the too near approach of the danger.

The Sand-piper is a solitary bird, and even when migrating he is independent of the rest of his kind, and faces the dangers of the voyage alone.

The nest is made of dry grasses in a hollow on the ground or under the shelter of a plant or tussock, and the four eggs are pale grey with spots and blotches of light and dark brown. They are big for the bird and she has to arrange them with the narrow, pointed ends towards the centre of the nest, to be able to cover them all at once.

PLATE XXXIV

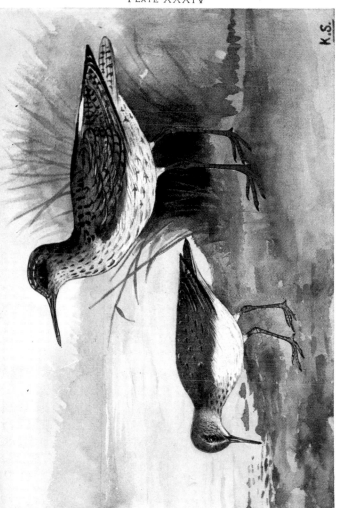

Sandpiper—(7½ inches)   Redshank—(12 inches)

PLATE XXXIV.

THE REDSHANK

THE Redshank is one of the commonest waders about our seacoasts, and he lives, too, about fens and muddy flats inland. He stays here all the year round and many come from further north for the cold weather, so that we have far more of these birds in winter than in summer.

The Redshank lives on worms and all sorts of small animals he finds about the seashore. With his long beak he digs deep in the sand for them. He has a very loud shrill note and calls out at any sign of danger, warning not only all the Redshanks near, but other kinds of birds too; for they understand his alarm-note very well. As he flies off you will see his white rump and the narrow white line round the curve of his wing, and perhaps his red legs.

The nest of the Redshank is placed in the shelter of a tuft of grass or under a low shrub, and is made of dry bents and lined with finer grasses. The four eggs are cream-coloured with markings of lighter and darker brown.

PLATE XXXV.

THE RINGED PLOVER

IN spring this pretty little bird may be seen about the banks of inland lakes and rivers, but at all other seasons he keeps to the sea-shore. Wherever a stretch of sand is left bare by the falling tide, a little flock of them may be found busily engaged picking up the worms and sandhoppers on which they live. They run very quickly a few yards, then stop, and then again run on. If you approach them quietly they run in front of you for a little distance, and if you still follow them, they rise into the air, wheel round over the sea and come back again not far from the place they have just left. The flight is rapid, and sometimes they all show the white feathers underneath, sometimes only the darker upper parts; and often the whole flock becomes suddenly invisible when the bright white is turned away as they sweep round in the sunshine. The nest is a simple hollow in the sand or shingle, in which four eggs are laid and arranged with the thicker ends outwards. They are buff or cream colour, with many black and grey spots.

PLATE XXXV

Ringed Plover—(7½ inches)   Moorhen—(13 inches)

PLATE XXXV.

THE MOORHEN OR WATER HEN

THE Moorhen or Water Hen, as she is often called, is a shy bird, but if not frightened away may become perfectly tame and friendly. Almost every quiet little sheet of water whose banks are fringed with rushes or osiers, has a pair of Moorfowl, and in the summer they may be seen any morning or evening swimming with their family in and out amongst the reeds. Most of their life is spent on or very close to the water, but they like to wander over grassy meadows, and sometimes they perch on trees. The white colour underneath, and a habit of giving little flirts with the tail, make it easy to recognise the Moorhen, even when you cannot see the red mark on the forehead and the red bands round the legs. They feed on water-insects, worms and grasshoppers, and are fond of grain and various plants. They can swim under water, and sometimes, when chased, they hide below the surface with only the bill sticking up through which to breathe. The nest is usually built among rushes beside water, but sometimes on a tree. Eight or ten brownish-grey eggs are laid, spotted with red-brown, and the mother covers them over with leaves when she goes away.

PLATE XXXVI.

THE PHEASANT

PHEASANTS are "game" birds; that is, it is a regular form of sport to hunt and shoot them, and they are used as food for the table. They are not native birds of this country, but were introduced from abroad hundreds of years ago. Even after all this time they are not quite at home here, and if left alone would get fewer in number and perhaps disappear altogether. The Pheasant requires to be protected against the cold hard winter, and supplied with food, and when the young birds are hatched they are carefully fed and their natural enemies driven away. Much money is spent every year in the breeding and rearing of young Pheasants for sportsmen to shoot when they grow up.

The cock Pheasant is a large handsome bird, with warm bright colours and a long slender tail, of which he is very proud. When he moves about, which he does in a leisurely fashion, with occasional little runs, he keeps it well up off the ground, and sometimes he lifts it up high as a Peacock does. He flies heavily with rapid beats of his wings, making a great fuss and noise when he is rising; but he can go very fast through the

PLATE XXXVI

Pheasant—(36 inches)

Hen

air when well started. He likes to live in the undergrowth of woods, among brambles, willows, long grass and low bushes, with occasional excursions to the hedgerows; and he much prefers to have water close at hand.

Pheasants are fond of all sorts of grain and do much damage to the farmer's crops. They also eat berries, acorns, and sometimes insects, especially ants and their eggs. The note of the Pheasant is a loud crow. During summer they roost on the ground at night, but in the winter, they fly up into a tree and roost in the branches.

The hen bird is much less handsome and conspicuous than the cock, and has not got the long tail-feathers. The nest is made of a few leaves and straws, and is placed in coarse grass or weeds, or under a hedge. The eggs vary from six to thirteen in number and are of a light olive-brown or green colour. The young birds learn to pick up their own food very soon after leaving the egg, and the cock Pheasant leaves the hen as soon as they are hatched.

PLATE XXXVII.

THE RED GROUSE

THE Red Grouse is the only bird that is not found in any country except Britain. He lives only in the north of England, Ireland and Wales; and all over Scotland he is common on the moors. He is a bird of the heather and the hills. In spring when you can approach quite near, you will see how handsome he is, with his red and brown feathers that suit his surroundings so well; and the chuckling crow with which he calls to his mate is a pleasant, cheery sound in these lonely places. Later in the year grouse go about in parties, which rise out of the heather at your feet with a startling rattle and whirr.

They live principally on young heather shoots, and on mountain berries and leaves. The nest is a slight hollow, scraped under a tuft of heather, and from five to twelve eggs are laid, dull white, blotched with reddish brown. The chickens very quickly learn to scuttle away under cover when danger threatens, or if they think they are being watched they lie still, trusting that their mottled plumage will not be seen among the heather.

Plate XXXVII

K.S.

Partridge—(13 inches)

Grouse—(16 inches)

PLATE XXXVII.

THE PARTRIDGE

THE Partridge is fond of cultivated country, and lives in stubble and grass, finding food chiefly in the fields. He is a common bird, and not shy. Partridges usually go about in flocks or coveys of from six to twenty birds, feeding and roosting together. At night they collect in some field, and the loud clear call-note uttered about sunset is familiar to everyone who lives in the country. They sleep in the centre of a field, forming a circle with all the birds facing outwards.

In spring they separate into pairs, and the nest is made in a corn-field or under a hedge. It is simply a hollow scratched in the soil and lined with grass. From six to eighteen eggs are laid of an olive-brown colour. The parents are very clever in protecting their young, and if you come near the nest the mother often tries to save them by fluttering and pretending to be lame and unable to fly, until you have followed her away from the chicks.

Partridges live on grain, seeds, insects and caterpillars. They are fond of taking a bath in the dust, and of sitting still, basking in the sun.

PLATE XXXVIII.

THE PEEWIT OR LAPWING

A STRANGE and beautiful bird is the Lapwing. He loves the free wide open spaces of the country, and makes his home on the moors and marshes, and stretches of uncultivated land. Wild as the waste he lives in, and shy and wary of the approach of man, he likes the society of his kind, and usually at least two or three are to be seen in the air together. In autumn, indeed, the Lapwings collect into very large flocks; but even in the breeding season several pairs make their nests near one another, and their cry is heard continually, day and night. It is a weird, wailing sound, this cry. It consists of two notes, and gives the bird its common name, for it is very like the two syllables "Pee-wit" or "Pees-weep," the second note higher than the first. On the lonely moor it is wild and melancholy, but is full of the sense of open air and freedom.

With his long crest and slender shape, the Pee-wit is very graceful, and his bright colours of green and red and white make him very beautiful. He runs quickly on the ground, and has a habit of stopping suddenly and lowering his head and shoulders as if balancing himself. In the air no

PLATE XXXVIII

Peewit or Lapwing—($12\frac{1}{2}$ inches)

other bird is like him, and you can always know him by his strange flight. The wings are short and rounded at the ends, and they flap slowly and heavily. For a few yards he flies forward, then suddenly he turns over and seems to tumble right down almost to the ground, then another turn and he is flying along close to the ground, or upwards, to descend again suddenly. He scarcely ever flies straight forward, but turns now to one side, now to the other, or downwards or upwards in the strangest and most whimsical fashion.

The nest is made of a few bits of grass or rushes placed in a hollow in the ground. The four eggs are arranged with the pointed ends inwards. They are usually dark green, blotched all over with brown, and Plovers' eggs (the Peewit is the green Plover) are very good to eat. The parents are very watchful and if you come near the nesting places, they come flying round your head in great alarm, crying and screaming, and trying to lead you away by pretending they are hurt.

They live on worms, slugs, and insects of various kinds, and feed even at night.

PLATE XXXIX.

THE CURLEW

THE Curlew has its name from its call. It is a clear ringing whistle of two notes, which can be heard from far away. In the springtime these two notes are repeated three or four times, and then prolonged into a rich, deep trill, repeated again and again. This call is one of the most wonderful sounds of all the bird-world. It is very wild, but rich and musical, with all the mystery and beauty of the lonely moors and hillsides that are the Curlew's home. It is a wild, eerie sound, so much so that in many parts of Scotland the "Whaup," as he is called, is held to be "unchancy."

Perhaps this idea is confirmed by his great wariness, and his alertness to notice the approach of danger when it is still far off. His call is an alarm for all the birds that feed near him on the long stretches of damp sand left uncovered by the falling tide. For the Curlew is one of the waders, and finds his food, sandworms and many small animals, in wet sand and marshes. For the greater part of the year he lives by the sea, going to the meadows and up to the hills at high water, and coming down to feed as soon as the falling

PLATE XXXIX

Curlew—(24 inches)

tide uncovers his prey. At those times small flocks live together.

But in the spring when the birds pair, they go to the moors, sometimes far inland, to build their nests. Then it is that the Curlew may be heard at his best. Sometimes if you walk up a lonely glen, your presence is enough to disturb several pairs, and they will fill the air with the haunting sound of this voice of the misty hills.

As the birds fly, you will see the barred white of the tail showing against the mottled brown of back and wings. And they are easily known by the long curved bill.

The nest of the Curlew consists of a few leaves roughly gathered together among long grass or heather. The four eggs are greyish green, mottled with brown and green. The young birds have quite straight bills at first. They quickly learn to run, and to squat flat down to hide from any danger.

PLATE XL.

THE SNIPE

THE Snipe is a bird of bogs and marshes. He cannot live in dry places because his food consists of the worms and creeping things that are to be found in mud. His long beak, with which he digs, is furnished with a soft, sensitive part at the end so that he can feel for his prey under the surface. As you can understand, a bird with such a bill cannot pierce the ground when it is hard with frost, and so many Snipe come here in the winter-time from colder places, and when it is very cold here they have to shift their ground and go to the seashore or to streams that do not freeze; or they go further south.

The Snipe is very wary, and difficult to get near. On the approach of danger, he will hide by lying close to the ground, where his black and brown mottled feathers are so like his surroundings of heather and other plants that grow about his boggy haunts, that he may often escape notice. If he is disturbed he will fly off up the wind, zig-zagging quickly from side to side in a way that is very puzzling to the sportsman who may be waiting to shoot him.

In early spring, and during the time the hen is

Plate XL

Snipe—(11½ inches)

sitting on the eggs, the cock performs an interesting flight, for her entertainment. He flies round and round, high in the air, now rising with quickly fluttering wings, now falling with wings outspread. And as he falls he makes a curious sound, called "drumming." No one quite knows how this sound is made, whether by the feathers of the wings or tail, as he sweeps through the air, or whether it is perhaps partly with his voice. It is somewhat like the bleating of a lamb, and the bird has been called "heather-bleater," in consequence.

The nest of the Snipe is placed among heather or rushes, and is made of dried grass and small pieces of dry heather. The four eggs, arranged in the nest with their narrow ends together, are yellowish, with mottlings of greenish brown of different shades.

PLATE XLI.

THE HERON

THE Heron is the largest of our common birds, and is to be found all over the country. Wherever there is water with fish in it, on the banks of broad rivers or tiny streams, by inland lakes or the shores of the sea, you may see him standing motionless, waiting for his food to come to him. He stands in the water, sometimes on only one of his long legs, sometimes on both, as if asleep. But watch him. Before long you will see a very slight movement of the head; he is taking aim; and then, all of a sudden the head and long bill are flashed into the water, and withdrawn with a small fish struggling in the beak. The capture is swallowed head first, and the Heron again settles down to another motionless spell. So successful is he that fishermen often carry a heron's foot in their pockets as a charm to attract fish. Sometimes when fish are scarce the Heron shifts his ground, but it takes long to tire him because he has a perfect patience.

It is easy to recognise the Heron's tall grey figure, as he stands on the shore; and it is also easy to recognise him when he flies. No other bird has the same motion of the wings, a steady,

Plate XLI

Heron—(38 inches)

heavy flap, so that he seems to be flying in the most leisurely way, even when he is going fast. His long legs are stretched out behind, and the neck is curved so that the head is close to the shoulders.   He can fly very many miles a day with those great wings.

Several Herons usually build their nests near one another, and a colony of this sort is called a " Heronry."   The birds come back to it year after year if not disturbed.   The nests are usually built in a tree, and as each nest is a very large, loose structure made of sticks, and there may be a great many nests on the same tree, a heronry is a curious sight.   Three or four eggs of a pale green colour are laid.   When the young are hatched they perch on the trees, and it is a comical thing to see a large grey bird sitting, as the young ones like to do, on the very top of a pine-tree, watching for the return of his parents with food.   The call of the Heron is a harsh, characteristic croak.

PLATE XLII.

THE WILD DUCK OR MALLARD

THE Mallard is a very shy bird, and you cannot easily get near enough to him to see his plumage of beautiful colours. As he flies at a distance, you may see the white ring round his neck, and the white and black on the wings, but you will not see the shining green of the head, nor the bar on the wings, nor the chestnut red of breast and neck.

Mallards are very common and live always near water, about lakes and marshy places, or by rivers; but they must be quiet, lonesome places, for it is only when driven by cold and hunger that Mallards will come near the dwellings of men. When the grain is ripe in the fields, however, they flock there at night to feed, and after the harvest they find food among the stubble. They also eat worms, small fish and insects, and grasses that grow by the water-side.

Flocks of Mallards live together, and a number may often be seen flying in a long slanting line, with a short quick flap of the wings, their long necks stretched out before them. The tail is very short.

The Mallard's nest is made in a dry place on the

PLATE XLII

Wild Drake—(24 inches)

Duck

ground, near water. It is of dry grasses with a thick warm lining of down.

When the duck has laid her ten or eleven greenish eggs and has begun to sit on them, the drake leaves her, and she has to hatch the eggs and take care of the ducklings alone. So when she has to go off to find food, and there is no one to take her place and keep the eggs warm, she plucks the down from her breast and lays it over them. The young ones can swim as soon as they are hatched.

The reason why the drake goes off at that time is that he begins to lose his feathers, and he probably feels very unhappy while that is going on, and cannot help to bring up the family. When the wing-feathers come out he cannot even fly till the new ones grow. The strange thing is that when he gets his new coat it is dull mottled brown, like the duck, and he has lost his brilliant colours. In the autumn he moults again, and then he puts on his bright coat once more.

PLATE XLIII.

THE CORMORANT

THE Cormorant is a very curious bird. On land, with his long neck and short tail he seems ungainly and awkward, and his staring, bright green eye gives him a wild, weird look. And on the sea he has odd ways of behaving which are very interesting to watch. He lives and fishes in fresh water sometimes, but the best place to see him is by the sea. There, on the wilder parts of the coast, there is often a solitary rock standing out alone above the water, known to the local fishermen as the Cormorants' rock. Usually several of them are there together. Some are sitting upright, facing the wind, with wings spread out as if to dry them, and so they will sit motionless for quite a long time. Others have their long necks straight out, with the beak raised as if swallowing something. Other birds keep coming and going to and from the rock. One will waddle to the edge and dive into the sea, and swimming under water, come up a long way off. Another comes flying in from a distance with a great beating of his wings like a Duck's flight, to join the group of sitting birds. It is a curious and interesting scene, and if the sun is

PLATE XLIII

Cormorant—(36 inches)

shining, the bright metallic blues and greens of the plumage make brilliant colours in the light.

The Cormorant is a strong flier, when he has started, although he has a difficulty in getting up from the water, flapping his wings on it with a prodigious bustle as he rises. But he flies long distances in search of food. He lives on fish, which he chases and catches under the water. Swimming with wings and feet, he can stay down a long time and move quickly after his prey. When he has caught a fish, perhaps a herring or mackerel, he comes up to the surface and swallows it head first. He is a very greedy bird. He has a habit of floating below the water with only his head and neck showing above; and sometimes one sees fifteen or twenty long necks close together, standing straight up out of the water, like so many floating champagne bottles.

The large nest is made of sticks and seaweed and grass, and is built on a rocky cliff or island. Three to five eggs are laid, long and narrow, and of a pale chalky colour.

PLATE XLIV.

THE OYSTERCATCHER

HAVE you not often seen a row of birds flying low over the water, side by side? They have chosen a particular wind-swept rock to rest on, and come up to it facing the wind and settle there to sleep till the tide falls. You go near enough and see their bright orange-coloured bills showing clearly against plumage of pure black and white; and the grey rock shows up the bright pink of their legs. Then you know that these are Oystercatchers, or Sea-pies as they are called, because they are black and white like the Magpie. Go nearer, and they will rise and perhaps go off silently further along the coast; but if any have nests or young there, they will wheel round over you, screaming pitifully, and sometimes making dashes as if they would like to strike you if they dared.

The nests are among the shingle or bents above high-water-mark; or perhaps in a slight hollow in the rock, where some broken shells and small white pebbles have been collected to line it, and to keep the eggs from any danger of lying in water. Indeed it is hardly a nest at all, and often the eggs are laid on the bare ground. There are

PLATE XLIV

Oyster Catcher—(17 inches)

three eggs, stone-coloured and blotted and streaked with dark brown. The little birds at first are covered with thick, soft down, mottled brown and white.

The Oystercatcher is one of the commonest birds about our sea-coast, and his loud clamouring is a familiar sound. He lives on shell-fish, as you may guess from his name. His bill is long and very powerful, and with it he knocks limpets off the rocks, when the tide uncovers them ; and mussels, too, and he prises them open, putting his bill between the two shells. At low-tide, too, he runs about the sand finding worms and insects. And sometimes, wading, he catches small fish. When the tide has covered the feeding grounds, large numbers of Oystercatchers may often be seen far inland. In winter they collect in big crowds, and many go from the further north parts of our islands southwards, while others come to us from other lands still colder.

PLATE XLV.

THE GULLS

OF all our sea-birds the Gulls are the most familiar. They are found all round our coasts at every season of the year, and great numbers of them live about the mouths of all our rivers. They spend most of their lives by the sea, but when the weather is stormy they come inland for shelter and you may often see them following the plough and picking up the worms turned up in the furrows. In winter some of them even follow the course of rivers for miles and miles inland. They are not very particular about what they eat. They live largely on small fish, which they catch as the shoals come to the surface, but they will eat almost anything that can be eaten, whether floating on the water or cast up by the tide. They follow steamers in the hope that something eatable may be thrown over, and they are wonderfully clever in seeing and picking up small scraps of food. On shore they eat insects, worms, grubs, and grain of all sorts.

There are many kinds of Sea-gulls, and it is not very easy to recognise them all as they congregate in screaming crowds over a shoal of small fry. When the tide is nearly full, you may

PLATE XLV

Blackheaded Gull—(17 inches)
Blackbacked Gull—(24 inches)

Common Gull—(18 inches)

perhaps see them sitting on the rocks at rest, and then you can make out the different kinds more easily. The Black-headed Gull with its red bill and legs is easily known, and so is the Black-backed Gull. Of the others in such a group, probably most are Common Gulls, with pearl-grey backs and black and white tips to their wings. The Herring Gull may also be there; he is very like the Common Gull, but is much larger and stronger. The plumage of young Gulls is usually a beautiful mottled brown, and all the Gulls change a little in winter. They have a harsh screaming note.

The Black-headed Gull makes its nest by some inland pond or marsh, building it of rushes, and lays three eggs, pale olive-green or brown with dark blotches. The other three Gulls named usually nest by the sea, often on the top of cliffs. The eggs of the Common Gull are yellowish-white with dark brown blotches. Those of the Herring Gull and smaller Black-backed Gull are very much alike, grey or brown, spotted and streaked with dark brown. The Black-backed Gull usually makes its nest on low islands.

PLATE XLVI.

THE GANNET

THE Gannet is often called the Solan Goose. He probably got this name because Gannets used to be sold in market-places for the sake of their down and feathers, and they are large white birds; but he is not really a Goose at all. All round the coast you may see him, and in all sorts of weather. His wings are very large, sometimes six feet from tip to tip, and very strong; and he can go on fishing alone in a storm, when the Sea-gulls have been driven to the shore for shelter. When fishing, he flies high above the sea, watching its surface till he sees one of the small fish he lives on. Then suddenly he drops, his wings half-closed and head first, right down, no matter how high he was, splash into the sea, sending up a white spray of foam. Catching the fish under water, he comes up to the surface, and after a moment's pause, rises again, to drop again in the same way for another. You can recognise him at any distance by this drop and splash, even when so far away that you cannot see the black tips of his long, white wings.

There are only about eight or nine places in Britain where Gannets make their nests, and there

PLATE XLVI

Gannet—(36 inches)

they collect in spring time, in tens of thousands. Most of these breeding spots are high, precipitous cliffs, on the ledges of which are collected the few sticks and pieces of grass or seaweed of which the nests are made. But they will build on the grass or turf at the top of the cliffs, if not disturbed. A Gannet's breeding place is one of the busiest and most interesting sights possible, the birds coming and going continually, pushing one another off the narrow ledges of rock to find room, and constantly calling and croaking in their hoarse, harsh voices. The parent birds fly huge distances in search of food, at this time, sometimes going fifty or a hundred miles in the day. One white egg is laid, and the shell is covered with a thick layer of chalk, which you can rub off. The old Gannet is all white except the forehead, chin and wing-tips, which are black, and the eye which is yellow, and the blue eyelids. The young birds are usually slate-grey, spotted with white.

PLATE XLVII.

THE TERN

EVERY bird has some interest or beauty of its own, and the Tern makes its special appeal to the eye, being particularly elegant in form and graceful in its movements. The pearl-grey of back and wings and the white of the under-plumage are contrasted beautifully with the velvety black cap, and the coral red of the bill and feet. The tail is long and forked, and the wings narrow, long and pointed, from which it has been given the name of "Sea-swallow." Like the Swallow, too, it is a warm-weather visitor, and comes to us at the beginning of May, heralding the summer.

The Tern breeds on low islands and rocky shores about our coasts, laying its three eggs in a slight hollow in the rock, or among shingle. They are buff or stone-colour, with blotches of dark brown and black. Any danger to the nests causes a very shrill clamour of protest; for the Tern has not a musical voice.

This bird feeds on fish, which it catches by diving. It hangs in the air, to take aim, then, with wings half-closed, drops into the water, like an arrow-head and just as fast. It stops on the surface only for a moment to swallow the fish it has caught, then rises again to search for more.

Plate XLVII

Manx Shearwater—(14 inches)

Tern—(13½ inches)

PLATE XLVII.

THE SHEARWATER

AS the Tern is a Sea-swallow so the Shearwater has been called the Sea-swift. His long, pointed wings are sooty black, and in flight he is strong and graceful. He has his name of Shearwater from his way of skimming the surface, first with one wing then with the other, turning to you now his white under-plumage and now his back. Sometimes he drops his feet and seems to paddle with them on the top of the water; for he is one of the "Petrels" who are named thus, "little Peter," because they seem to walk on the water, like the apostle.

Shearwaters live entirely on the water except in the spring, when they dig burrows, for nests, in sandy or peaty soil at the top of sea-cliffs. Very many of them used to breed on the Isle of Man, hence their name of Manx Shearwater. During the breeding season the Shearwater spends much of the day in his underground home, fishing at night and in the evening and early morning. But when the one white egg is hatched and the young bird fledged, they all go back to the sea.

PLATE XLVIII.

THE GUILLEMOT

THIS bird lives entirely on the open sea. It can dive and swim under water, using both wings and feet, and at the approach of any danger it pops under to hide. Only to lay and hatch its one egg does the Guillemot leave the water, and for that purpose it chooses a steep rock or cliff overhanging the sea, where thousands and thousands live together. No nest is made, but the egg is of such a shape that it cannot roll off the rocky ledge on which it is placed. It is broad and round at one end and very pointed at the other, and when the wind blows, it just turns round on one spot. The bird does not sit on it to hatch it, but stands over it, placing it between her feet where the tail feathers keep it warm. The egg of the Guillemot varies very much and may be any colour from white to deep green or blue, with or without spots and blotches. When the little bird is fledged it is taken down to the sea by its parents, and calls plaintively when they disappear under the water searching for fish for it. The old birds say "wurra-wurra" in a low tone, with a louder "urrr-r-r" when they are anxious or excited.

PLATE XLVIII

K.S.

Puffin—(12½ inches)　　　　　Guillemot—(18 inches)

PLATE XLVIII.

THE PUFFIN

THE Puffin is a very odd-looking little bird indeed, owing to his large red and yellow bill. His figure is neat and compact, and the plumage all black and white, so that his bill looks even larger than it is, because of its bright strong colours. It is shaped somewhat like a parrot's, and the bird is often called "Sea-parrot."

The Puffin is a summer visitor to our coasts and breeds in thousands about rocky islands and cliffs. For its nest it chooses a hole in a rock; or it will turn a family of rabbits out of their hole and lay its egg there; or it will make a burrow for itself, digging a tunnel of several feet in length, and at the end of that a collection of feathers forms the nest. The egg is white, sometimes with faint grey markings. To feed the young bird, the clever Puffins sometimes bring as many as a dozen fish at a time, the tails hanging out at both sides of their beaks.

At all other times of the year the Puffin lives at sea, swimming and diving much more easily than it can walk on shore.

WHERE TO FIND THE BIRDS

IN GARDEN OR SHRUBBERY

Missel-thrush	Greenfinch	Nightingale	Nuthatch
Song-thrush	Bullfinch	Willow-wren	The Tits
Blackbird	Goldfinch	Hedge-sparrow	Pied Wagtail
Sparrow	Whitethroat	Flycatcher	Starling
Chaffinch	Redbreast	Wren	

IN FIELD OR HEDGEROW

Missel-thrush	Linnet	Yellow Bunting	Jackdaw
Song-thrush	Redbreast	Corncrake	Magpie
Blackbird	Hedge-sparrow	Cuckoo	Wood-pigeon
Sparrow	Flycatcher	Meadow-pipit	Pheasant
Chaffinch	Wren	Starling	Partridge
Greenfinch	Common Bunting	Rook	Sparrow-hawk
Whitethroat			

ON MEADOW OR COMMON

Missel-thrush	Swallow	Yellow Bunting	Jackdaw
Goldfinch	House-martin	Cuckoo	Barn Owl
Linnet	Pied Wagtail	Skylark	Kestrel
Flycatcher	Wheatear	Meadow-pipit	Pheasant
Wren	Stonechat	Starling	Partridge
Swift	Common Bunting	Rook	Peewit

IN THE WOODS

Redbreast	Nuthatch	Magpie	Sparrow-hawk
Nightingale	Tree-creeper	Jay	Pheasant
Willow-wren	The Tits	Wood-pigeon	Heron
Wren	Cuckoo	Barn Owl	

ON MOOR OR MOUNTAIN SIDE

Wren	Meadow-pipit	Grouse	Curlew
Wheatear	Kestrel	Peewit	Snipe
Stonechat	Golden Eagle		

BY LAKE OR RIVER

Sedge-warbler	Sand-martin	Dipper	Snipe
Snipe	Pied Wagtail	Sandpiper	Heron
Swallow	Grey Wagtail	Redshank	Wild Duck
House-martin	Kingfisher	Moorhen	Seagulls

BY THE SEASHORE

Rock-pipit	Redshank	Curlew	Oyster-catcher
Starling	Ringed-plover	Heron	Gulls
Sandpiper			

OUT AT SEA

Gannet	Oyster-catcher	Shearwater	Guillemot
Cormorant	Tern	Gulls	Puffin

INDEX

112